REBOUND
RESTART
RENEW
REBUILD
REJOICE

TIMOTHY OTTE

Cover photograph by Katherine Scott © 2008.
Design & layout by Kyle Harvey.

REBOUND, RESTART, RENEW, REBUILD, REJOICE
TIMOTHY OTTE
ISBN 978-1946-583-093
Lithic Press

LITHIC PRESS
fine books for an old planet

www.lithicpress.com

For my brother, Joey
For my sister, Katie

REBOUND
RESTART
RENEW
REBUILD
REJOICE

Beginning in the late 1880's   *1*
        The Canadian Pacific Shoreham
Facility was used for myriad
        Railroad activities. My family

History is mostly unknown to me.   *5*
        I am a fourth-generation St. Paul
Resident on my mom's side. I grew up
        Near my mother's childhood home, and not

Far from where my grandfather was raised. I
        Know little of your upbringing, but I   *10*
Know that you and my mother married in
        1985. Thirteen years later   *In May*

You and she parted ways, your lives like tracks
        That ran briefly parallel. Part of the
Roughly 230 acres   *15*
        Were leased to occupants who conducted

A range of activities including
        Chemical storage and distribution.
The Shoreham Facility's opera-
        Tions began about half a century   *20*

After the surrounding land was stolen
        From the Indigenous population
Of the area, the Dakota and
        Anishinaabe peoples, following

The Land Cessation Treaties of 18-   *25*
        37. I was never taught this
History. I don't know how our fami-   *Not really, not well*
        Ly settled in Minnesota. How did

They reckon with the violence? I wish
        I knew. I was always told that I would   *30*   *I live on stolen land*
Understand our family's break up when
        I grew up. Older now, I know adults

Sometimes become directionless. I know
     It's not my business. Still, you exist twice:
Once, here in the present, and again as   *35*
     A ghost, a bird. Something unreachable.

Something distant. The U.S.–Dakota
     War of 1862 further con-
Solidated Indigenous land in
     Colonial hands at the expense of   *40*

Thousands of lives. Our history is filled
     With spills: blood, oil. Historical activ-
Ities on the Shoreham Facility's
     East side resulted in soil and ground-

Water pollution in various zones.   *45*
     You dislike nebulous statements like this
And challenged me to communicate well,
     Especially in writing. You said, Be   *"You'll always be in demand if*
                                                you can write."

Specific. You said, I no longer want
     To be married to your mother. I still   *50*
Remember the chair you were sitting in.   *Forest green with a small,*
     That morning, I had woken early with   *cream fleur de lis pattern*

A bloody nose. Your words staunched the flow like
     Yarrow. Later, I went outside to ride
My bike as far and fast as I could,   *55*
     As if my exertion could halt our lives,

Slow us and keep us on the tracks I had
     Always known. However, I never got
To ride my bike. It had been stolen out
     Of the garage. Contamination on   *60*

The Site includes petroleum-rela-
     Ted pollution and solvent-related
Volatile Organic Compounds, also
     Known as VOCs. The house we lived in

At the time was angular and unreal,   *65*
      A blend of truth, half-remembrances,
And dreams. I can hardly trust my own mind.
      Memories nestle other memories

Inside of them. I'm convinced the house was
      Haunted, but maybe only because, when   *70*
I was young, I wished it had been haunted.
      Is the house haunted now with my ghosts, my

Memories? Canadian Pacific
      (CP) and Ashland, a former tenant
Of the property, are developing   *75*
      And implementing the soil and ground-

Water cleanup. Over the last fifteen
      Years, I've written several versions of
This poem. I tried to write it like all
      My other poems, crowded with the things   *80*

I hide you behind, but when I tried, I
      Ended up writing a whole book, and not
This poem at all. Then, this week, the poem came
      As a newsletter, sent by CP and

This poem first drafted in August 2014

Ashland about a cleanup being con-   *85*
      Ducted on a commercial train yard near
My apartment. Oversight of the work
      Is provided by the Minnesota

Pollution Control Agency (MP-
      CA), where you worked when I was a kid.   *90*
This is the work you do. This newsletter
      Contains words you might write, mixed here
          with mine,

Double helix of science and poet-
      Ry. I looked at this letter because I
Thought that we could talk about it. You could   *95*
      Tell me what you know about the project,

About the land and its long history.
> This is the type of thing I could ask you
About. In September 2003,
> We fell out. My angst spilling across the   *100*

Facility of your home. I walked out
> And later said I no longer wanted
To see you. Let us both apologize
> For our mistakes. I'll go first: I'm sorry.

I'm sorry

In August of 2005 I was   *105*
> Happier than I'd yet been in my life.
I had removed you from it, ignoring
> The problem of our soured relationship.

Things were simpler as a result. You had
> Been out of my life for two years. I was   *110*
In love for the first time. That month, CP
> And Ashland presented an RAP

(Response Action Plan) which was approved by
> The MPCA on January
20th, 2006. I was   *115*
> About to turn eighteen when approval

Passed. The Shoreham Facility is in
> Excess of 200 acres, but clean
Up of VOC contamination
> Is in progress on a tiny fraction   *120*

Of the Site: The Former Lease Area,
> The Roundhouse Area, and The Former
Waste Reclamation Area. For three
> Years I've lived two blocks south and four
>   blocks east

On stolen land

Of the Site. I walk by sometimes when out   *125*
> With my dogs. It's fenced in, chain link and
>   bleached
Wood keep the curious from wandering
> Too close to the trains, but signs facing the

Street describe the site and work being done.
      Two years ago, when my house was teeming   *130*
With them, I caught a mouse and released it
      On a service road that runs along the

A former apartment—now,
all the mice are killed

Site. Since April 2006, a Soil
      Vacuum Extraction (SVE) system
Installed by Ashland has operated   *135*
      As part of the soil cleanup. That June,

I graduated high school and fled the
      Nest, landing among trees in another
River valley. You called to say you were
      Proud. I think you sent a card and a check,   *140*

Which I cashed, without thanks. Four months later,
      In October, you wrote a letter and
Mailed more money: The total funds of an
      Account for my education. We talked

For no more than five minutes in the months   *145*
      After my graduation, but I've saved
All of your letters, or most of them at
      Any rate. There's enough pain in them to

Blister. There's a lot of truth in them, too.
      I see that now. Perhaps you knew I would.   *150*
Writing this poem is part art-making,
      Part history project. I'm learning as

Part archive, part meta-
memoir

Much about myself as I am about
      The Site. I have primary sources to
Set alongside the secondary source   *155*
      Of my own memory. Maybe you can

And emotions to layer on all
of it

Annotate this poem to provide more
      Data. Writing this is a way for me
To set down our history, to remem-
      Ber it. Free product (also known as Light   *160*

Annotate my annotations

Non-Aqueous Phase Liquid, LNA-
        PL) is also being removed from
Several wells using absorbent socks,
        Bailing, and a Non-Aqueous Extrac-

Tion Technique (NET™) system that has   *165*
        Removed roughly 231
Gallons of LNAPL to date.
        I'm sipping tea and water as I write.

The water is warm and straight from the tap.
        Something is off with our plumbing—when I   *170*
Turn on the cold tap, hot water flushes
        From the boiler, forcing cold water

Into the pipes. The next time we turn on
        The hot faucet, cold water gushes out.
The water looks and tastes fine, but sometimes   *175*
        I think that we should get a filter. It

Would make the tea better, not that it's bad.
        Deeper groundwater contamination
Is being addressed by a pump system,
        Which began operation in July   *180*

2007. I was dating
        Someone older than me, and I was just
Beginning to see the cracks between us.
        I wasn't writing very much. I have

Two poems from that time, both talking to   *185*
        A higher power I'm not so sure I
Believe in, each poem seeking wisdom,
        And each poem uncomfortable with

Certainty, but wishing for certitude.
        I was nineteen years old, flailing around   *190*
For some notion of selfhood, trying on   *I'm still flailing around*
        Attitudes and ideas like clothing.

Extracted groundwater is treated on-
    Site using granular activated
Carbon before being discharged into   *195*
    A sanitary sewer under a

Permit from the Metropolitan Coun-
    Cil Environmental Services. Since
Then, you've remarried, renovated your
    House, adopted several sweet cats, and   *200*

Roughly 2,300 pounds
    Of water contamination have been
Removed and treated. No graph can chart your
    Marriage though it seems to be trending up.

Again, it's not my business. I used to   *205*   *Since this poem was drafted*
    Tell myself I'd never do what you did,   *you've gotten divorced again*
But I don't know what mistakes to avoid.
    As I get older, I get better at not

Comparing myself to others. I am
    Not you, no matter how many of your   *210*
Genes I carry. I am sure I will make
    The same mistakes as you, unknowingly.

CP installed SVE systems to
    Remove contamination in the earth
Under the Former Roundhouse Area,   *215*
    The Former Shops Area, and Former

Waste Reclamation Area. Full-scale
    Operation commenced in April of
2007. You got married
    In September 2007.   *220*

I wasn't invited and found out months
    Later, when I heard about it from my   *After reading this the first*
Siblings, who mentioned it casually   *time you wrote to say I'd been*
    Over dinner, as if it was a known   *invited*

Fact, expected. They said that you proposed   *225*
        Over dinner, too, saying that getting
Married was your New Year's resolution.
        I don't know if that's true, but it's true in

Its own manner. The lived truth is a wave
        To the particle of my memory.   *230*
The groundwater contamination is
        Being addressed by pumping from wells lo-

Cated southeast of the Roundhouse. Again,
        It occurs to me to ask if drinking
From my tap is unsafe. I imagine   *235*
        You laughing and saying, The water's fine,

                                                          The water is fine

You're safe—it's the air quality you have
        To worry about. I would promise to
Bike more, eat less dairy. I've given up,
        You'd say. You have said. I'll be dead by the   *240*

Time we see the worst effects. You're almost
        Casual about environmental
Collapse, a cynical, but rational
        Response given your line of work. You see

A lot of messes and meet a lot of   *245*
        People who are uninterested in
Cleaning them up. The well system began   *And yet, I'm struck by the*
        Operating full-time in November   *fact that you keep doing the*
                                                          work

Of 2007. Extracted
        Water was initially pre-treated   *250*
Prior to discharge. Five months later you
        Turned forty-seven and laid your mother   *Grandma Rita*

To rest. She'd "gone to glory" as she had
        So often said and you so often quote.
At her funeral, we occupied space   *255*
        Together for the first time in over

Five years. The funeral home was tense. I
      Remember the way everybody grew
Quiet and looked at me when I entered.
      I went to you right away, to prove to   *260*

You, them, and myself that I had grown up.
      Looking back, five years is not all that long,
But accounted, at the time, for a quar-
      Ter of my life. We still hadn't sorted

Out our issues, but you wrote later to   *265*
      To say that you were "encouraged" that I was
Able to have a "normal chat." It would
      Be two more years before our roots grew back.

Or maybe they didn't. Perhaps there's just
      Sod over the topsoil of our lives.   *270*
Maybe you'll read this. Maybe we will pull
      Out our buckthorn, fertilize new prairie.   *You have read this*

Treatment of contaminated soil
      And water below the water table
Using bioremediation be-   *275*
      Gan at pilot scale in December of

2007. Just under a year
      Later, in October 2008,
I broke down in South Dakota, hundreds
      Of miles from home. I have to wonder   *280*   *Thanks to MT, MH, MS,*
      and SG for their support

If that collapse was triggered by our re-
      Connection the prior spring. The stress of
Reconciliation and relearning
      How to live with you as part of my life

Was as baffling as quantum physics, too   *285*
      Much for me to process. I broke down in
The hands of a gentle and quiet man,
      Father of a friend, my borrowed father,   *Thanks also to MT's parents*

Who let me smoke his cigarettes and cry.
        Deadwood felt like a house, the town so small   *290*
And close that each building felt like a room.
        In the months leading up to that collapse,

My vision became narrow. Everything
        I looked at was focused, severe, and bright.
Every object looked at, felt, discarded.   *295*
        It couldn't last. I should have seen ruin

Coming. Later, I visited the grave
        Of Calamity Jane, frontierswoman—
The Patron Saint of Bad Decisions—just
        Outside of Deadwood. I left her whiskey   *300*

And a cigar. Mother Calamity   *I still pray to her*
        Who visited my life and mucked my dirt.
In November of 2009
        I was mostly stable, dealing with my

Neuroses and sadness with therapy.   *305*
        That month MCES approved direct
Discharge of extracted and treated ground-
        Water to the sanitary sewer.

That autumn, I started meditating
        And exercising again after a   *310*
Summer of hard work and harder drinking.
        I was beginning to think I may live   *I'm still recovering from that summer*

To see adulthood. It had never crossed
        My mind that I might have a life I could
Really like. To date, approximately   *315*
        341 pounds of V-

OCs have been removed, and here I am,
        Twenty-seven years old and surprised to
Be alive. The pilot trial of the   *Thirty years old now*
        Bioremediation treatment was   *320*

Completed on February the 12th,
     2010, two days before I turned
Twenty-two. You gave me a novel by
     Nicholson Baker about a poet,

And wrote a sweet card. I still have the card   *325*
     And the book and I always think of you
When I see it. In *The Anthologist*,
     Baker's narrator has a theory re-

Garding iambic pentameter that
     Is fascinating, if a little cracked—   *330*
A broken pentameter. Later that
     Spring, when I graduated from college,   *A broken pentameter*

You took me out to a nice dinner to
     Celebrate. Afterward, you opened the
Hatch of your battered minivan to re-   *335*
     Veal an old typewriter, the very same

Smith-Corona you'd had for forty years.
     It's one of the best gifts I have ever
Received, and was a wonderful statement   *Still*
     Of support for my writing. Following   *340*

MPCA approval in July,
     Bioremediation began in
October 2010, the month
     That M. and I met. Our first date was on

Halloween. Almost five years on, we are   *345*
     Living together. She is my partner   *We recently celebrated seven*
In all things, supportive, assertive, and   *years and now have two dogs*
     Beautiful, and also the child of   *together*

Divorced parents. I love her family
     As much as ours. Destruction of contam-   *350*
Inants is being enhanced by adding
     Nutrients and a commercial bio-

Remediation culture which helps to
        Degrade the chlorine-based solvents to non-
Toxic end products. Every time we talk   355
        I think, This is a good thing. We degrade

The toxicity between us. You said,   *Is this metaphor too heavy-*
        I don't know why you left. You said, Maybe   *handed?*
You needed to focus your resentment
        Somewhere and I was the best target. That's   360

Probably close to the truth, but, ten years
        On, I'm still not sure I know. Reading your
Letters now, all that pain crawls back into
        My throat. I admire your use of words

And narrative structure. I remember   365
        You once said that you wanted to be a
Writer. Do children live out the dreams our   *Will you write a poem for*
        Parents abandoned? Do you have these let-   *me? I don't care if it's bad*

Ters saved somewhere, or were they lost in moves
        Or a decade of spring cleanings? You said, 370
A partnership takes two people to make
        It work just as it takes two people to

Make it fail. Is that true? Or is that a
        Way of passing the blame? That aside, there's
Truth in your letters. It sears my skin. It   375
        Burns and burns and burns. SVE systems   *It burns and burns and*
                                                       burns

Ran constantly to extract VOCs
        Until May 2011 when
Removal rates reached asymptotically
        Low levels. That year, I was trying to 380

Decide what to do with my life. I was   *Not that I now know what I*
        Working part-time when proposals to start *want to do*
Rebound/restart cycling (consistent with
        The RAP) were submitted to the

MPCA. I was trapped beneath a   *385*
    Mountain of debt, hemmed in, living with my   *Am still trapped*
Mom, stuck between feeling like a child and
    An adult. I was uncomfortable.

That spring we started meeting frequently
    To talk, beginning the long process of   *390*
Patching things up. We apologized to
    One another. We finally started

Healing. Restoration. A Monitored
    Natural Attenuation approach
Was selected as the remedy for   *395*
    The deep bedrock aquifer. The five-year

MNA monitoring period
    Was completed in 2012.
In January of that year I was   *And finally starting to write*
    Writing about life as an additive   *400*   *some good poems*

Process. I was thinking about adding
    School back into my life. I was thinking
About a future, or not, with M. She
    Was applying to schools too and we weren't

Certain our relationship could survive   *405*
    If both of us were focused on school in   *I didn't go to school, she*
Different parts of the country. I was   *did—and we're still together*
    Starting to realize how in love I

Was. Monitoring data has reli-
    Ably shown ongoing degradation   *410*
Of contamination. The earth has start-
    Ed to put itself back together. Here,

At least, is a bit of hope about the
    Future. It's small, but it is hope, feathered
And singing. It tells us that we can fix   *415*
    Our toxic selves. It tells us we can change.

Residents near the site get their water
       From the City of Minneapolis
Municipal drinking water system,
       So the groundwater contamination   *420*

Doesn't pose a risk of exposure. This
       Doesn't explain the warm water in the
Cold tap of my kitchen sink, but does make
       Me more comfortable drinking what comes

Out. Still, I would like to get a filter.   *425*
       Rebound/restart cycling operated
Through August 2013. That's when
       I began working on a book, which led

Me to this poem. This poem shifted
       The work of the book. I never set out   *430*   *And the work of the book*
To write a confessional. I'm worried   *changed the work of this*
       About forcing our relationship to   *poem*

Conform to some sort of narrative, since
       What I enjoy about being your son
Is being constantly surprised, and how   *435*
       What I know about you is in constant

Flux. Stories demand an ending and our
       Relationship doesn't end. It goes on.   *May it go on a long time*
Almost 2,550
       Pounds of VOCs have been removed by   *440*

SVE systems from the Roundhouse and
       Shops Area and approximately
129 pounds from the
       Former Waste Reclamation Area.

2013 was a good year,   *445*
       The beginning of an upward trend in
My life. I wake up most days surprised by
       My circumstances. How content and how

Consistent I must look from the outside!
      A confirmation Dirt and Soil-Gas *450*
Sampling Work Plan was approved by the M-
      PCA on October 21st,

2013 with sampling beginning
      The next month, around which time M. and I
Threw a party. You and your wife came, but *455*
      Left before my mom arrived. Your exit

And her entrance timed to avoid unease.
      It was easier for you to not see   *Will everything always be*
One another, but it was still the low   *uneasy for you both?*
      Point of the party for me, the only *460*

Moment that our shared history broke in-
      To the bright comfort of the gathering.
Since installation, the Soil Vacuum
      Extraction system has removed almost

5,980 pounds *465*
      Of VOCs from the soil. Last year,
An additional monitoring point
      Was installed to audit shallow soil

Vapor. Also last year, I moved into
      A new apartment, where I've written the *470*   *We still live in the same*
Entire text of this poem. This house   *apartment*
      Is a few blocks from another place where

I lived with a roommate. M. and I now   *On stolen land*
      Live with a small menagerie of pets.
We try to balance each other's strengths and *475*
      Weaknesses. She's a good cook, so I wash

Dishes. We leave each other notes about
      Plans and just to say hi. It's not perfect,
But we're happy and stable and planning
      A future together. My last few years *480*

Have been some of my best. I've been driven
         And productive—the usual darkness
Of depression and anxieties has
         Been manageable. I've built a life and

Since writing this poem, I
started a new job I love

A supportive network of good friends. I   *485*
         Never knew this was possible and feel
Fortunate to know I'll always have these
         People in my life. Petroleum clean-

Up at each of the ten leak sites has been
         Completed to the satisfaction of   *490*
The MPCA. Nonetheless, in the
         Interim, removal and recycling

Of free product (diesel fuel) will con-
         Tinue in the Former Collector Pan
And Former Pump House Areas. My life   *495*
         Is less of a mess these days. I try to

Be aware when the potential to make
         Mistakes with M. is great. She shows me how
To be a better partner, a better
         Person, more giving and careful of the   *500*

May I always continue to get
better at these things

Needs of those around me. Moving forward,
         We expect continued operation
Of SVE systems in the Former
         Ashland Lease Areas, in addition

To LNAPL collection. I   *505*
         Might get dinner or take the dogs for a
Walk to look at the Site through the chain-link
         Fence. Completion of the Soil cleanup

In the Roundhouse Area, Former Shops
         Area and the Former Waste Re-   *510*
Clamation Area. We can expect
         Rain tomorrow, and cool temperatures

Flux

Into next week. I catch sight of myself
　　　　In the mirror and see your profile, your
Mouth. I sound just like you when I make jokes　　　515
　　　　Or laugh. I have your smile. Continued

Operation of water extraction
　　　　And treatment systems. I'll go to sleep and
Dream of a time I no longer feel like
　　　　I'm on the verge of spilling over or　　　520

Dropping something precious. Continued growth
　　　　Of self, continued learning. M. and I
Occasionally talk about getting
　　　　Married, but we aren't yet sure. We both have　　　*And what would a wedding*
　　　　　　　　　　　　　　　　　　　　　　　　　　　　change for us?

Other priorities before we make　　　525
　　　　That decision. I'd like to publish a
Book, she'd like to find full-time work. We're both
　　　　Happy with our arrangement, our easy

Life of art and pets and a cozy home
　　　　Together. Continued monitoring　　　530
Of full-scale bioremediation
　　　　At the Former Lease Area. The Site

Will never be the same, at least in my
　　　　Lifetime. Like us, the land we inhabit
Is in constant flux, it shifts and vibrates.　　　535　　　*Flux and text*
　　　　We're fragile and fallible, but we can

Change, we can survive. This is where I live:
　　　　Train tracks pressed into the earth. Ghosts. A
　　　　　　home.
Memories nested inside memories.
　　　　Questions, comments? Please feel free to　　　540
　　　　　　contact.

NOTES

"Rebound, Restart, Renew, Rebuild, Rejoice" is after Timothy Donnelly's "Hymn to Life." The poem interpolates text from the 8th annual East Side Shoreham newsletter prepared by Canadian Pacific and Ashland Inc. and published June 2014. Additional reports and other information are available at www.shorehamrepository.com.

Additional information is from treatiesmatter.org, usdakotawar.org, and native-land.ca.

ACKNOWLEDGEMENTS

This poem was revised in a studio at Open Book thanks to support from The Loft Literary Center's Mentor Series in Poetry and Creative Prose. Thanks to my mentors and peers, especially Matt Rasmussen, April Gibson, Kate Lucas, and Rhea Davidson, and program manager Sherrie Fernandez-Williams.

I'm also indebted to Éireann Lorsung and Jennifer Kwon Dobbs, who are mentors who have become friends and colleagues. Their guidance and light have been instrumental.

Andrea Sanow helped with revisions and is my favorite person to talk with about writing.

Thank you to my dad for working so hard to rebuild and for not only allowing the poem, but rejoicing in it.

And Molly: thank you for being in the poem, for being next to me, for your love.

Timothy Otte is a poet and critic. Poems have appeared in *Denver Quarterly, Sixth Finch, Fence, SAND Journal, Reservoir* and elsewhere. Reviews have appeared in the *Poetry Project Newsletter,* and on *Colorado Review, LitHub,* and *Chicago Review of Books,* among others. He was a 2014–15 Loft Mentor Series winner and a fellow at the 2017 Poetry Incubator. Otte keeps a home on the internet: www.timothyotte.com. Say his last name like *body*.